W9-BZG-534

Barack Obama

ROBIN S. DOAK

Children's Press®
An Imprint of Scholastic Inc.
New York Toronto London Auckland Sydney
Mexico City New Delhi Hong Kong
Danbury, Connecticut

Content Consultant
James Marten, PhD
Professor and Chair, History Department
Marquette University
Milwaukee, Wisconsin

Library of Congress Cataloging-in-Publication Data

Doak, Robin S. (Robin Santos), 1963–
  Barack Obama/by Robin S. Doak.
     p. cm.—(A true book)
  Includes bibliographical references and index.
   ISBN 978-0-531-21904-1 (library binding) — ISBN 978-0-531-23875-2 (pbk.)
 1. Obama, Barack—Juvenile literature. 2. Presidents—United States—Biography—Juvenile
literature. I. Title.
  E908.D63 2013
  973.932092—dc23 [B]   2012036050

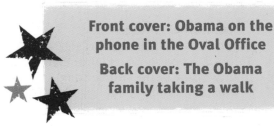

Front cover: Obama on the phone in the Oval Office

Back cover: The Obama family taking a walk

Find the Truth!

Everything you are about to read is true *except* for one of the sentences on this page.

Which one is **TRUE**?

T or F Barack Obama was the first African American to run for president.

T or F Barack Obama appointed the first Hispanic judge to the Supreme Court.

Find the answers in this book.

Contents

THE BIG TRUTH!

The Obama Family

Obama's grandparents give him a hug after his high school graduation.

Obama's first administration loaned millions of dollars to struggling U.S. car companies.

CHAPTER 1

The Early Years

In 2008, Barack Obama became the 44th president of the United States of America. His election had a special significance. After decades of struggle for equal rights among African Americans, he was the first to be elected president. But President Obama's story did not begin with the 2008 presidential election. It actually began almost 50 years before, on an island chain in the middle of the Pacific Ocean.

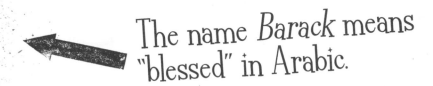

The name *Barack* means "blessed" in Arabic.

Young Barack

Barack Hussein Obama Jr. was born in Honolulu, Hawaii, on August 4, 1961. His father, Barack Obama Sr., was from Kenya in Africa. His mother, Stanley Ann Dunham, was from Kansas. Barack's parents had met while attending college in Hawaii. When Barack was just 2 years old, his mother and father separated. Not long after, his parents divorced.

Barack Jr. was named after his father (pictured here).

As a boy, Barack was known as Barry.

Barack is pictured here with his mother, stepfather Lolo, and his sister Maya.

Ann later married Lolo Soetoro, a college student from Indonesia. In 1967, Lolo, Ann, and young Barack left Hawaii and settled in Jakarta, Indonesia. Barack spent four years there. He learned how to speak Indonesian and attended school. His mother made sure he remembered his American roots. She woke him at four o'clock each morning to study English before school. She also taught him about African American leaders such as Martin Luther King Jr.

Barack spent much of his childhood living with his grandparents until graduating high school.

Home to Hawaii

When Barack was 10 years old, he was accepted at the elite Punahou School in Honolulu. He moved back to Hawaii, where he lived with his grandparents, Stanley and Madelyn Dunham. Both were important role models for Barack, who taught him to work hard and always think for himself.

Ann and Maya, Barack's baby half sister, soon came to Hawaii. The three lived together until 1975, when Ann and Maya returned to Indonesia so Ann could study there. Barack stayed in Hawaii with his grandparents.

In high school, Barack was smart, friendly, and high-spirited. He played on the school's varsity basketball team. He helped his team win the state championship in his senior year. Barack was also known as an excellent debater, and he wrote for the school's journal. He graduated from Punahou in 1979.

Barack's teammates nicknamed him Barry O'Bomber for his powerful jump shot.

11

College Days

Obama spent two years at a university in Los Angeles, California, before transferring to Columbia University in New York City, New York. In 1983, he graduated with a degree in political science. In college, Obama became interested in **civil rights** and working to improve life in poor communities. After college, he took a job on the South Side of Chicago, Illinois. There, one of his tasks was to help people who had lost their jobs.

Barack became interested in working with poorer communities while living in New York.

Visiting Kenya

Obama saw little of his father when he was growing up. Yet he was very interested in his African roots and relations. In 1987, Obama made his first trip to Kenya, his father's homeland. During the trip, he met his step-grandmother, aunts, uncles, and some of his seven half brothers and half sisters. He also visited the grave of his father, who had died in a car crash in 1982.

A Rising Star

Obama spent three years studying at Harvard Law School. After graduating in 1991, he returned to the place he now considered home—Chicago. Obama taught law at the University of Chicago and worked hard for the city's residents. He fought for civil rights by helping thousands of African Americans register to vote. He also began to make a name for himself as a hard worker and as someone who could get things done.

Obama was the first black president of Harvard Law School's journal, the *Harvard Law Review*.

A New Family

In Chicago, Obama met a smart, young lawyer named Michelle Robinson. Michelle had been born and raised in the city. The pair had much in common. Like Obama, Michelle had attended Harvard. She was also interested in helping people in poor communities. The two fell in love and were married in October 1992. They later had two daughters, Malia and Sasha.

Michelle and Barack met when she was his mentor, or guide, at a Chicago law firm.

Michelle and Barack Obama pose on their wedding day with their mothers.

Obama worked to gain support for new laws on health care and other issues while serving in the Illinois Senate.

Into Politics

During the early 1990s, Obama was an active member of the Democratic Party in Illinois. His hard work there paid off in 1996, when he was elected to serve as an Illinois state senator. He was elected to the job two more times, serving a total of eight years. As a state senator, Obama focused on important issues such as health care and workers' rights.

Losses and Wins

In 2000, Obama set his sights on Washington, D.C. That year, he ran for U.S. representative to Congress. He lost, but he learned important lessons on how to run a campaign and win people's votes.

In 2004, Obama ran again for national office. This time, he set his sights on the U.S. Senate—and he won by a landslide. He gained 70 percent of the total vote to defeat his Republican opponent.

A Timeline of Barack Obama in Chicago

1985
Obama takes a job with Developing Communities Project in Chicago, Illinois.

1989
Obama meets Michelle Robinson while working as an intern for a Chicago law firm.

The victory made Obama the nation's only actively serving African American senator. Soon after his election, Obama gave a speech at the Democratic National Convention. He spoke of all Americans as one people, united by their love for their country. The speech earned him a standing **ovation**. It also energized people across the country. Obama was now the Democratic Party's rising star.

1992
Obama teaches law at the University of Chicago.

1995
Obama writes a book about his father. His mother dies the same year.

1996
Obama wins his first term in the Illinois State Senate.

2004
Obama is elected to the U.S. Senate.

CHAPTER 3

A Promise of Hope and Change

Just two years after becoming a U.S. senator, Obama traveled to the Old State Capitol in Springfield, Illinois. There, on a cold winter day, he announced that he would run for president of the United States. Obama faced a tough battle. Many people thought he didn't have the experience that other candidates had. But in the coming months, he would convince Americans that he was the right person for the job.

Abraham Lincoln and Barack Obama announced their first presidential campaigns at the same location.

The Nomination

Obama's first challenge was to convince Democrats to choose him as their **nominee**. Several other Democrats wanted this honor, too. All of Obama's opponents had more political experience than he had. All of them had served as senators or governors. But Obama's message of hope gained him many young supporters. His promise to change the way things were done in the national government appealed to people of all ages.

Obama's campaign appealed to many young voters.

Obama, vice presidential nominee Joe Biden, and their wives appear at the 2008 Democratic National Convention.

In August 2008, Democrats from around the nation met in Denver, Colorado, at the Democratic National Convention. There, they chose Obama as their candidate for president. Obama accepted the nomination before a record-breaking crowd of some 50,000 people. Millions of Americans watched the historic moment at home on their televisions. Obama wasn't the first African American to run for the office. Several others, such as Congresswoman Shirley Chisholm and the Reverend Jesse Jackson, also ran for the U.S. presidency. But Obama was the first to gain a major party's nomination.

John McCain speaks at a campaign rally with his running mate, Sarah Palin (left), and his wife (right).

The Election

At the convention, Obama chose Senator Joe Biden of Delaware to be his vice presidential **running mate**. Now, the two faced off against Republican candidates John McCain and his running mate, Sarah Palin, governor of Alaska. McCain was a **veteran** of the Vietnam War (1954–1975) and a longtime Arizona senator. During debates, he told voters about his years of experience in the government.

Obama focused on his message of hope and change. Many of his campaign volunteers were young Americans. They used the Internet to reach other voters and raise money for Obama's campaign. The Internet helped Obama's message spread quickly across the nation. On November 4, 2008, people all across America voted. By the end of the day, Obama had won the election.

Obama received more than 69 million votes, the largest total number ever received by a single candidate.

The Obama Family

President Barack Obama knows that he can count on his family for support and love.

First Lady Michelle Obama was born in Chicago, Illinois, on January 17, 1964. The president calls her his rock. As first lady, Michelle travels around the United States, encouraging kids to exercise and eat healthy foods.

Malia Ann Obama was born on July 4, 1998. Malia takes dance lessons and can play the piano. She and her sister, Sasha, attend a private school in Washington, D.C.

Natasha "Sasha" Obama was born on June 10, 2001. Sasha loves to tap dance. She also takes gymnastics and piano lessons.

Bo is the newest member of the Obama family. He came to live at the White House in April 2009, when he was six months old. Bo is a Portuguese water dog.

CHAPTER 4

President Obama

On January 20, 2009, Barack Obama was sworn in as the 44th president of the United States. People around the world watched as the first African American president in U.S. history took the oath of office. Obama knew that he faced many tough challenges. The U.S. economy was suffering. In 2008, 2.6 million people lost their jobs. Could the new president make a difference?

Obama took the oath of office with President Abraham Lincoln's Bible.

Spreading Peace

One of Obama's first actions as president was to strengthen the nation's relationships with other countries. He promised leaders around the world that the United States would work with them to solve international problems. He also focused on bringing peace to the **Middle East**. This region has long suffered from war and conflict. Obama also pledged to work to eliminate nuclear weapons around the world.

Obama met with many international leaders, including Crown Prince Mohammed bin Zayed Al Nahyan (center) from the United Arab Emirates.

U.S. troops and other international forces were still active in Afghanistan even after most troops had left nearby Iraq.

During his presidential campaign, Obama had promised to bring U.S. troops home from Iraq and Afghanistan. Troops had been fighting in those countries since the early 2000s. Between 2009 and 2011, American troops were withdrawn from Iraq. The conflict in Afghanistan was harder to end. As of May 2012, about 87,000 soldiers remained in the war-torn nation. That month, Obama announced the last troops would be home by the end of 2014.

The availability of health care in the United States has been a topic of debate for decades.

Health Care

Another top priority for Obama was health care. In 2009, about 50 million people in the United States had no health insurance. One out of every 10 American children had no insurance. Another 25 million Americans had some insurance but not enough. These **underinsured** people could not afford to pay their medical bills. In 2009, Obama proposed a health care bill. Obama believed the new bill would make insurance more affordable.

Most Democrats in Congress supported the president's health care plan. But most Republicans opposed it. Opponents believed that it was not the job of the government to fix the health care system. In late March 2010, after heated debate, Congress approved the bill. Obama signed it into law days later. The new law would provide insurance to more people and put tighter rules in place for insurance companies.

Obama signed the health care bill into law on March 23, 2010.

The Economy

The biggest challenge that President Obama faced was fixing the U.S. economy. When he took office, the economy was the worst it had been in 25 years. The number of poor Americans had grown larger. The number of people without jobs continued to climb. Banks and other companies were failing. The American people had little confidence that things were going to get better.

Thousands of Americans visited job fairs and employment offices to look for work in the 2000s.

Obama signed bills that helped keep U.S. carmakers in business.

One month after becoming president, Obama took action. He worked with Congress on improving the economy. In the coming years, the Obama administration pushed for tax cuts to provide struggling Americans with more spending money. The president also signed laws that tightened up rules for banks and other financial companies. The new rules made people's **investments** safer. Things improved, but very slowly.

Each year, the president gives a State of the Union address to talk about how the country is doing and his plans for the coming year.

CHAPTER 5

Challenges and Triumphs

During his first two years in office, President Obama made many changes. But not all Americans were happy. Some people thought that Obama had gone too far with his health care law. Others believed that the president's economic plan had increased the amount of debt in the United States. In the coming months, Obama's popularity would decline.

George Washington gave the first State of the Union address in 1790.

International Actions

In 2011, civil war broke out in Libya. The nation's leader, **dictator** Muammar Ghaddafi, was killing Libyans who protested against his government. Obama soon ordered U.S. Navy troops to fire missiles into Libya in an effort to help end the conflict. Several other nations around the world also took part in the efforts to stop Ghaddafi. Fighting ended in October 2011 after Ghaddafi was killed. But unrest still continued in the country.

Citizens throughout Libya rose up against Muammar Ghaddafi in 2011.

Obama and his cabinet watched the bin Laden raid as it took place.

On May 2, 2011, the hunt for the world's most wanted terrorist came to an end. That day, President Obama announced that Osama bin Laden was dead. Bin Laden was the leader of the terrorist group al-Qaeda. He planned the attacks against the United States on September 11, 2001, that left nearly 3,000 Americans dead. For 10 years, bin Laden had avoided capture. After learning that bin Laden had been found in Pakistan, Obama approved a raid on the location by U.S. troops. Bin Laden was killed during the resulting gunfight.

Obama often hosts large dinners to welcome international leaders and other visitors.

Presidential Perks

The job of being president is a difficult one. But many parts of the job are satisfying and fun. The president travels around the world to meet other nations' leaders. He also entertains important and interesting people in the White House. On one day, he might welcome the queen of England or the president of China to his home. Another day, he might host a Super Bowl–winning football team.

Two New Judges

During his time in office, Obama appointed two new justices to the U.S. Supreme Court. In spring 2009, he nominated Sonia Sotomayor. She is the first Hispanic judge to be part of the nation's highest court. The following year, he chose Elena Kagan to serve on the court. Today, three of the nine Supreme Court justices are women—the most ever to serve at one time.

Seated, from left: Associate Justices Clarence Thomas and Antonin Scalia, Chief Justice John Roberts, and Associate Justices Anthony M. Kennedy and Ruth Bader Ginsburg. Standing, from left: Associate Justices Sonia Sotomayor, Stephen Breyer, Samuel Alito Jr., and Elena Kagan.

Obama's Last Election

In May 2012, Obama kicked off his campaign for reelection. He faced a steep challenge to win the following November. His Republican opponent, Mitt Romney, blamed Obama for the still-shaky economy. It was a hard-fought campaign. The Obama and Romney teams spent billions of dollars on ads, Web sites, and other campaign efforts. The candidates also participated in three debates about important issues.

Obama and his family pose for a picture at the White House.

Obama (left center) and Vice President Joe Biden (right center) celebrate their 2012 election victory with their wives beside them.

On November 6, 2012, slightly more than half of all voters chose Obama. The president would stay in the White House for a second and final term. After his win, Obama acknowledged that the next four years would not be easy ones. But he also told Americans that he was hopeful. He promised, "Something better awaits us so long as we have the courage to keep reaching, to keep working, to keep fighting." ★

Day Obama was born: August 4, 1961

Place where Obama was born: Honolulu, Hawaii

Name of Obama's parents: Stanley Ann Dunham Obama (1942–1995) and Barack Obama Sr. (1936–1982)

Universities Obama attended: Occidental University, Columbia University, Harvard Law School

Name of Obama's wife: Michelle LaVaughn Robinson (born 1964)

Names of Obama's children: Malia (born 1998); Natasha (called Sasha, born 2001)

Occupations Obama had before winning the presidency: Community advocate, law professor, politician

Titles of books written by Obama: *Dreams from My Father; The Audacity of Hope*

Did you find the truth?

F Barack Obama was the first African American to run for president.

T Barack Obama appointed the first Hispanic judge to the Supreme Court.

Resources

Books

Gormley, Beatrice. *Barack Obama: Our 44th President*. New York: Aladdin Paperbacks, 2012.

Rhatigan, Joe. *White House Kids: The Perks, Pleasures, Problems, and Pratfalls of the Presidents' Children*. Watertown, MA: Charlesbridge Publishing, 2012.

Uschan, Michael V. *Michelle Obama*. Detroit: Lucent Books, 2010.

Visit this Scholastic Web site for more information on Barack Obama:
★ www.factsfornow.scholastic.com
Enter the keywords **Barack Obama**

Important Words

civil rights (SIV-uhl RITES) — the individual rights that all members of a democratic society have to freedom and equal treatment under the law

dictator (DIK-tay-tur) — a person who has complete control of a country, often by force

investments (in-VEST-mints) — things to which someone has given money, time, or effort in hopes of getting something back

Middle East (MID-uhl EEST) — a region that is part of Africa and Asia and made up of Egypt, Iran, Iraq, Israel, Saudi Arabia, Syria, Turkey, and other nearby countries

nominee (nah-muh-NEE) — someone who is suggested to run in an election, to fill a job, or receive an honor

ovation (oh-VAY-shuhn) — a response with loud applause and cheering

running mate (RUN-ing MAYT) — a person who runs for public office with another candidate in a less important position

underinsured (uhn-dur-in-SHURD) — having some insurance but not enough to pay the total cost of a medical bill

veteran (VET-ur-uhn) — a person who has served in the armed forces, especially during a war

Index

Page numbers in **bold** indicate illustrations

About the Author

Robin S. Doak has been writing for children for nearly 25 years. A graduate of the University of Connecticut, Robin loves writing about history makers from the past and the present. She lives in Maine with her husband, two dogs, and a cat named Lumpy.

PHOTOGRAPHS © 2013: AP Images: 38 (Alexandre Meneghini), 27 center (Carolyn Kaster), 26 inset (Charles Dharapak), 20 (Charles Rex Arbogast), 13 (Darko Bandic), 24 (Gerald Herbert), 31 (Hoshang Hashimi), 33 (J. Scott Applewhite), 8, 19 left (Obama for America), 5 top, 9, 10, 12 (Obama Presidential Campaign), 41 (Pablo Martinez Monsivais), 34 (Paul Sakuma), 22 (Rick Bowmer), 23, 28 (Ron Edmonds); Dreamstime/Jean Schweitzer: 26 background, 27 background; Getty Images: 11 (Laura S. L. Kong), back cover (Mandel Ngan/ AFP), 6 (Mark Wilson), 27 top (Marvin Joseph/The Washington Post), 17 (Phil Velasquez/Chicago Tribune/ MCT), 43 (Scott Olson), 14 (Steve Liss/Time Life Pictures); Newscom/Douliery Olivier/Abaca: 25; Polaris Images: 16, 18; REX USA: 3, 27 bottom, 36, 44; Shutterstock, Inc./Mesut Dogan: 19 right; Superstock, Inc./ Flirt: 32; White House Photo/Pete Souza: cover, 4, 5 bottom, 30, 35, 39, 40, 42.